A

COPY OF THE LAWS

OF

HARVARD COLLEGE,

1655.

With an Introduction

By SAMUEL A. GREEN, M.D.

A

COPY OF THE LAWS

OF

HARVARD COLLEGE,

1655.

With an Introduction

By SAMUEL A. GREEN, M.D.

CAMBRIDGE:
PRESS OF JOHN WILSON AND SON.
1876.

A COPY OF THE LAWS

OF

HARVARD COLLEGE, 1655.

THE following copy of the laws of Harvard College, in 1655, appears to have been given to the library in the year 1799. It has recently been found among the papers of a deceased member of the Society, and been returned by one of his family. According to the memorandum written on the cover, this copy was "presented to the Histor[l] Society, 1799, by John Pinchon, of Salem"; and this is the only record in regard to the manuscript. It comprises fourteen pages of closely written paper, of duodecimo size, the last two pages being in a different handwriting and on different paper. The first twelve pages seem to have been more used, and are considerably torn and worn about the edges. These have been placed in a double paper cover, of which one leaf at the back contains the two pages in the different hand. At the end is written "Admittatur Jonathan Mitchellus in collegiū Harvardinū 22. 8. 1683. Jn[o]. Rogers. P[r]ses. Samuel Andrew" [Socius]. From this it would appear that it was given to Jonathan Mitchell, a graduate of 1687, on his admission as a Freshman. It was the custom then, as it is now, for each student, on entering college, to have a copy of the laws, though now it is given to him in print. At that time, he was obliged to procure it himself; and, as paper was scarce, it is likely that the body of the pamphlet was sometimes handed down from one generation of students to another, and constituted a kind of *transmittendum*. Under such circumstances, it was natural that there should be verbal variations in the laws, as they were sometimes written by different hands. As the students graduated, their copies were frequently put in new covers, and, with the addition of the last two pages including the "Admittatur," &c., taken by the Freshmen.

The figures in the brackets show where the pages in the manuscript begin.

In the "Old Colony Memorial" (Plymouth, Massachusetts) for June 3, 1875, a similar code of college laws is published, which was also in force in 1655. It varies considerably in language from the one in the possession of the Society, though there is no great difference between them in the general tenor.

The lawes of Harvard Colledge agreed upon by the Overseers, President, and fellowes. Many of them in former yeares at severall times, and the rest more lately, but all of them, (as they hereafter follow) received ratified, and concluded upon at a meeteing of the overseers, President and fellowes of the said Colledge on the 30 *day of the second month.* 1655.

First concerneing admission and manners of students, as also toucheing theire expences In the Colledge.

1. When any Scholler is able to read and understand Tully, Virgill or any such ordinary classicall authors, and can readily make, speake, or write true latine in prose, and hath skill in makeing verse, and is competently grounded in the greek language, so as to be able to construe and grammatically to resolve ordinary greek, as the greeke testament, Isocrates, and the Minor Poets or such like, haveing withall meet testimony of his towardness, he shall be capable of his admission Into Colledge, and every Scholler shall procure for himselfe a true coppy of the lawes, which being signed with the Presidents and one of the Fellows hands shall be a testimony of his admission into colledge, and also of the time thereof which he shall keepe with himselfe for his better guidance, whilst he shall continue a member of the college. Every one shall consider the maine of his life
which is to know God and Jesus Christ [2] [and] answerably to lead an honest sober godly life.

3. Every one shall so exercise himselfe in reading the scriptures twice every day, that he shall be ready to give an account of his proficiency therein, both in theoreticall observations of Language and logick, and in practicall and spirituall truths, as his tutor shall require according to theire severall standings respectively, seeing the entrance of the word gives light. Psalmes 119, 130.

4. All Students shall eschew the profanation of gods name, attributes, word, or ordinances and times of worship, and in the publick assemblies they shall carefully eschew what soever may shew any contempt or neglect thereof: and be ready to give an account to theire tutors, of theire profiteing, and to use such helps of storeing themselves with knowledge as theire Tutors shall direct.

5. They shall honour as theire naturall Parents, so also magistrates, elders, The President, Tutors, fellows and all superiors, keepeing due silence in theire presence, and not disorderly gainesayeing them, but

sheweing all those laudable expressions of honour and reverence that are in use, as uncovering the head and the like.

6. All Students shall be slow to speake and eschew and in as much as in them lies, shall take care, that others may avoid all sweareing, lieing, curseing, needless asseverations, foolish talkeing. scurrility, babling, filthy speakeing, chideing, strife, raileing, reproacheing, abusive jesting, uncomely noise, uncertaine rumors, divulging secrets, and all manner of troublesome and offensive gestures, as being the [*torn*] should shine before others in exemplary life. [3]

7. No scholler shall goe out of his chamber without coate, gowne, cloake, and every one every where shall weare modest and sober habit, without strange ruffian like or new fangled fashions, without all lavish dress, or excess of apparel what soever: nor shall any weare gold and silver or such ornaments, except to whome upon just ground the President shall permit the same, neither shall it be lawfull for any to weare long haire, locks, or foretops, nor to use curling, crispeing, parteing or powdering theire haire.

8. No undergraduate upon any pretence of recreation or any other cause whatsoever, (unless allowed by the President or his Tutor) shall be absent from his studies or appointed exercises in the Colledge, except halfe an houre at breakefast, an houre and halfe at dinner, and after evening prayer untill nine of the clock: but while he is in the Colledge he shall studiously redeeme his time, both observing the houres common to all the Students to meet in the hall, and those that are appointed to theire own lectures, where unto he shall diligently attend, being inoffensive in word and gesture.

9. No Student shall goe into any Taverne, vittaileing house, or Inne to eate or drink, unless he be called by his parents, Guardians, or without some sufficient reason such as the President or his Tutor may approve of: neither shall any one entertaine any stranger to logde or abide in the Colledge, unless by the leave of the President or his Tutor, or in case of theire absence of one of the fellows: neither shall he without sufficient reason such as the President or his Tutor shall approve, either take Tobacco or bring or permit to be brought into his chamber strong beare, wine, or strong water or any other enebriateing drink, to the end that all excess and abuse thereof may be prevented.

10. No Student shall under any pretence whatever use the company or familiar acquaintance of persons of ungirt and dissolute life, [4] intermeddle with other mens buisiness, nor Intrude himselfe into chambers, neither may any undergraduate goe out of the town, nor be present at any Courts, Elections, Faires, Traineings, or any such like assemblies, except upon leave obtained of the President or his Tutor, or two of his fellows in theire absence.

11. No Student shall board or lie out of the Colledge, without just cause allowed by the President, nor shall any stay out of the Colledge after nine of the clock at night, nor watch after eleven, nor have a light before four in the morning, except upon extraordinary occasions.

12. Every undergraduate shall be called onely by his sur name unless he be the son of a nobleman, or a knights eldest son, or a fellow commoner.

13. Every fellow commoner shall bring a peice of Silver plate to the Colledge to the value (at the least) of three pounds with his name engraven thereupon, which he may have the use of while he shall abide in the Colledge, and shall leave it to the propriety of the Colledge when he departs from it.

14. Every Student that is an undergraduate shall be bound to continue in the Colledge, excepting upon weighty occasions made known to the President and his Tutor and with theire consent and notwithstanding his discontinuance shall pay halfe the Tuition.

15. Every discontinuer shall beare a share in Colledge detriments; viz.

16. He shall pay after five shillings a quarter for the removall of those many distractions and great burdens of labour, care and cost that heretofore have pressed the steward, and the great debts that hitherto sundry have run into, and unsutable pay, whereby the house hath been disappointed of sutable provision, occasioning inoffensive complaints. It is therefore provided.

1. That before the admission of any Scholler, his Parents or freinds shall both lay down one quarters expences, and also give the colledge Steward security for the future, [5] and without this Ingagement no Scholler shall be admitted into the Colledge.

2. That all such payments shall be discharged to the Steward of the Colledge either in the currant coine of the country, or wheat or malt, or in such provision as shall satisfie the steward for the time being, and supply the necessitie of the Colledge.

3. That who soever is Indebted to the Colledge at the end of any Quarter (besides his being liable to the course of the law for the recovering the debt) he shall have his stewards bill given in, and in case the bill be not paid within a moneth he not being suffered to run any farther into debt by expences, untill his whole debt be discharged.

4. The Students that now have studies in the Colledge shall pay for them the accustomed rent, but all that are hereafter admitted shall pay rent to the Colledge quarterly for theire chambers, and studies as they shall be valued by the President and fellows. likewise where as certaine summs of money have been set upon the students heads for the building of the gallery in the meeting house (for which the Colledge is Indebted) It is provided that each student that shall be admitted hereafter shall pay 3 shillings four pence for the use of the said gallery at theire admission which they shall be charged withall without any repaiment.

8. [*sic*] It is also ordered that for the charges of his commencement each commoner shall pay three pounds.

2ly: Lawes about holy duties Scholasticall exercises and helps of learneing.

1. Seeing God is the giver of all wisedome, all and every Scholler besides private prayers (where in every one is bound to ask wisedome) shall be present morneing and evening at [6] publick prayers at the

accustomed houres; viz: ordinarily at six of the clock in the morneing, from the tenth of March at Sun riseing and at five of the clock at night all the yeare long.

2. It is appointed that part of the holy Scripture be read at morneing and evening prayer, to wit, some part of the old testament at morneing and some part of the new at evening prayer on this manner: Thatt all Students shall read the old Testament in some portion of it out of Hebrew into greek, and all shall turne the new Testament out of English into greeke, after which one of the Bachelors or Sophisters shall in his course Logically analyse that which is read, by which meanes both theire skill in logick, and the Scriptures originall language may be Increased.

3. All undergraduates shall publickly repeat sermons in the Hall in theire courses, as also Bachelors untill they have commonplaced that so with reverence and love they may retaine god and his truths in theire minds. Also the Students shall be commonly examined in the last day of the week at evening prayer, and give an account of theire profitting by the sermons the week past.

4. A scholler shall not use the English tongue in the Colledge with others schollers, unless he be called thereunto in publick exercise of oratory or the like.

5. In the first yeare after admission for foure dayes of the week all Students shall be exercised in the Studies of the greek and Hebrew tongues, onely beginning logick in the morneing towards the latter end of the yeare: unless the Tutor shall see cause by reason of theire ripeness in the languages to read logick sooner. Also they shall spend the second yeare in Logick with the exercise of the former Languages and the third yeare in the principles of Ethicks, and the fourth in [7] metaphisicks and mathematics, still carrying on theire former studies of the week for Rethorick, oratory and Divinity.

6. It is appointed that in the teacheing of all arts such authors be read as doe best agree with the Scripture truths, wherein the speciall care of the President and fellows shall be used and theire direction therein attended.

7. All Students in the Colledge shall observe theire course in disputation: Bachelors once a fortnight, and the undergraduates such as have read logick, twice a week, excepting two moneths for the commencers before and a fortnight after the commencement for all the Students. Likewise all undergraduates shall declaime once in two moneths the number of declaimers being so divided that in the space of two moneths all may constantly declaime, excepting onely the times afore mentioned.

8. There shall be a Common place handled in Divinity once a fortnight, the President beginning and the Masters of Art and senior Bachelors following according to theire seniority: wherein the President and fellows take care that heretick opinions and doctrines may be avoided and refuted, and such as are according to the analogie of faith be held forth and confirmed.

9. To the Intent that the progress of learning amongst the Schollers

of the Colledge be yearly made known unto and Incouraged by meet Judges: All Questionests shall sit in the Colledge Hall on the second and third days of the third weeks next followeing the summer Solstice from nine of the clock till eleven in the foornoon and from one till three in the afternoon to be examined by any according to the law hereafter provided for such as are to commence Bachelors: also in case of eminent defect or notorious Insufficiency in any student by experience found or known by the President and fellows they signifieing this to six [8] or seven of the overseers with theire consent the deserveing may be preferred according to theire merit, and the Insufficient placed with such as better further theire progress in learning.

10. Every Scholler that upon proofe is able to read extempore the pentateuch of [or ?] the new testament into latine out of the originall tongues, and be skilled in logick, and competently principled in naturall and morall philosophie and the mathematicks, and also of honest life and conversation, and at any publick act hath the publick approbation of the overseers, and president of the Colledge, he may be Invested with the first degree: but ordinarily besides such approbation none shall expect it, untill they have been four whole yeares in the Colledge, or three yeares and 10 moneths at the least, being blameless and attending upon and performeing in theire courses all publick exercises or otherwise If they be discontinuers approved as before, and in matters of learning and manners qualified as continuers.

11. What Bachelors soever shall present unto the President a written Synopsis or Compendium of logick, naturall philosophy morall philosophie, Arethmatick, Geometry, or Astronomy within a week of the summer Solstice in his third yeare after his first degree, which Synopsis shall be kept in the Colledge Library and shall be read to defend his propositions, and be skilfull in the originall tongues as afore said, haveing stayed three yeers after his first degree, and therein thrice problemed, twice declaimed, and once made a commonplace, or else some answerable exercises to the studies that he is most conversant in, and remaineing of a blameless conversation, and the President of the Colledge, shall be capable of his second degree, viz; to be master of Arts. [9]

Thirdly concerneing penall lawes.

1. There shall be appointed a generall Monitor that shall observe them that are faileing, either by absence from prayers or sermons, or come tardy to the same, which shall bring weekly a catalogue of the names of delinquents to the President which Monitor shall be allowed a stipend of three pounds per annum for this paines of his, which shall quarterly by equall division be set upon the heads of all the undergraduates whose names are in the Buttery.

2. Each Student that shall absent himselfe from prayers (there being no Just reason given to and allowed by the President for such absence) shall for the first offence, being absent more then once or comeing tardy more then twice in a week space be punished a penny a time for once absent or twice tardy.

3. If he offend again in the like kind within a fortnight, he shall be nonplusht so many daies as he hath been absent from the duties of Gods worship and comeing twice tardy to prayers, and being once absent from sermons, It shall be accounted of as twice absent from prayers.

4. If this shall not work reformation in him or them, but within a fortnight he shall so offend againe, It is appointed that for the next offence any such delinquent or delinquents shall be publickly admonished before the Students of the Colledge, and the admonition with the time thereof noted by the Butler. If this shall not work reformation in him or them, but that within another fortnight he or they shall offend again in the like manner It is appointed that every such delinquent shall make publick confession of his offence a written forme prescribed by the President which shall also be recorded by the Butler.

5. If any shall refuse to make such conf[ession] [*torn*] confession of his offence sha [10] [*torn*] profanely negligent within a moneths time, [the]n he shall be suspended from his seniority, and the priviledge thereof at meales and for a weeks time or more according to the nature of his offence.

6. If he shall continue in manifest obstinacy and contempt of authoritie, and of meanes of reformation, then It is appointed that by the notes of all or the major part; viz: of the President and fellowes such an one shall be expelled out of Colledge, which condition, shall be attended still in all the after lawes concerning expulsion.

7. Each undergraduate that shall neglect to read sermons in his course shall be nonplusht two dayes and lose his commons one meale for such neglect, and the dutie shall still lie upon him, and his continued neglect thereof shall be punished according to the gradation of penalties in the former lawes.

8. Also in case any student shall be negligent to repaire to lectures in the Colledge with the rest of his classis: It is appointed such negligent persons. be carefully observed by theire tutors, who shall send for any such students and admonish them before the rest of his classis.

9. For the second offence his Tutor shall complaine to the President who shall publickly admonish him. & after such admonition and no reformation there upon, the President shall appoint him a publicke confession (as before) of his offence.

After this If it manifestly appeare, he reforme not thereby the Pluralitie of the notes of the President and fellowes (due patience being used) he shall be expelled out of the Colledge.

Every student that shall neglect the performing of any Scholasticall exercise in his course, shall [for] the first offence by the President or his Tutor [be] appointed to make Double exercise, or some scholasticall exercise, [besi]des the performance of that which was omitted.

[If he sh]all still refuse the exercise, then he shall [be suspende]d from his seniority as above; and If he were the lowest of his classis before for his [11] learnings sake he shall performe exercises with the rest of his classis, but be put below some of the n[ext] classis in sitting.

3. If he continue negligent, then such neglect shall be punished with the loss of seniority in his classis such as he had before.

4. If the former course prevaile not to work more paines and diligence in the party, It is further appointed that such wilfull neglect shall be punished with degradation from his classis, and the loss of a yeares time.

5. If thereupon no reformation should follow, then after a moneths patience by the pluralitie of notes of the President and fellows such a shamelese non perficient shall be expelled out of the Colledge.

6. If any undergraduate shall depart out of the Hall at dinner or supper before thanks be given without just cause, or the leave of the senior fellow that shall be present in the Hall, he shall lose his commons so many meales, as he shall so offend: also they that needlesly frequent the Kitchen shall be non plusht by the President.

7. If any Scholler shall abide out of the Colledge or be absent from his studies beyond the times before allowed, either spending his time in any house or place of the town, or goeing out of the town without the leave of the President or his Tutor, or haveing leave of the President or his Tutor, shall without cause stay longer then his appointed time; he shall for such offences be nonplusht by the President and his Tutor, and tasked to make some scholasticall exercise by the appointment of the President.

8. No undergraduate shall buy, sell, barter, or exchange books, apparrell or any thing of considerable value; but by the leave of the President or his Tutor, Guardian or Parent, or If he shall sell or pawne any thing to any scholler, the President shall make the bargaine and admoni[sh] [12] [the] student noe students shall be suffered to have [a g]un in his or theire chambers or studies, or keepeing for theire use any where else in the town, or If they be found to have such by the President or Theire Tutors, then they shall be admonished by the President or theire Tutors to put it away: which If they shall refuse to doe, the President shall have power to take it quite away from them, and If they resist the President herein, they shall upon due proofe be expelled out of the Colledge by the advise of the Colledge overseers: the same penalty is appointed to any student that shall make resistance against or offer violence unto the President or fellows.

10. If any Student shall weare long haire, or other wise offensive contrary to the former seventh law the President shall have power to reforme it, or as need shall require to make his address to any three or more of the overseers, who shall take order concerning it.

11. It is appointed that every Student that shall by good evidence be convicted of any hainous and flagitious crime, As Robbery, Burglary, Speakeing blasphemous words, notorious profanations of the lords day, ordinances or word, uncleanness or such like, shall be expelled Ipso facto, and in case that any be convicted of drunkeness, fighteing, raileing, sweareing, curseing, filthy speakeing, profaness, reveling, playeing at cards and dice, or such like, for the first offence If it be private, he shall be privately admonished by the President or his Tutor; and for the second offence If it be publick he shall be publickly admonished by the President; and for the third shall make publick [con]fession of his offence at some publick [meeting?] of the

Students, and for the fourth [offence shall be n]oted down for a prophane person. [13] having his commons sitting in the Hall uncovered, & if upon this he reform not & make not some expression of sorrow & repentance after a months triall & patience he shall be expelled out of the Colledge.

12. It is provided that in such gross offences, as attaines to the lawes aforesaid are punishable with expulsion, It shall be in the liberty of the president & fellowes to inflict corporall punishment by the rod (as a degree anteceeding expulsion according to the condition of the offender, & nature of the offence.

13. Concerning the penalties abovesaid It is provided that if any of the prescribed degrees of punishmēt do work reformation, then whatsoever degrees of punishment have been passed before, shall be made void in order to any further censure.

14. It is required of every Colledg officer or Servant that he be faithfull in discharging the place, & trust committed to him, so as may tend to the welfare of the Colledge & of all the members thereof, & in case of unfaithfullness, negligence, or any other miscarriage in his place, he shall be accountable to, & punishable by the President & fellowes to the quality of ye offēce.

All These Lawes upon publishing openly in the Colledg Hall shall be of force immediately.

At a meeting of the overseers ye 30 day of ye 3^d^ month For as much as the overseers have been certified that there hath been uncomfortable defects in the diet of the students as also in their lodging: It is ordered that the Corporation speedily inquire into the causes [14] thereof, & take order wth the Steward & Treasurer or any other Colledg Officer, whom may concern for the just redress of the same, & the Overseers do promise their best assistance for the effecting of it, wch may be needfull.

Another penall Law is exacted by the generall Court held at Boston; ye 17 of ye 8 month 1656 & published in the audience of the Students in ye Colledge.

It is hereby ordered that the President & fellowes of Harvard Colledge, for the time being, or that the major part of them are impowred to punish all misdemeenours of the youth in their Society either by fine or whipping openly in the Hall as the nature of the offence requires not exceeding 10 shillings or 8 stripes for one offēce & this law to continue in force untill the Court or Overseers of the Colledge provide some other orders for

Such offences.

ADMITTATUR JONATHAN
MITCHELLUS in collegiū Harvardinū
22. 8. 1683. JN^o^. ROGERS. P^r^ses.
SAMUEL ANDREW.

www.ingramcontent.com/pod-product-compliance
Lightning Source LLC
LaVergne TN
LVHW020638110826
845149LV00004B/1266

* 9 7 8 1 4 1 8 1 8 9 6 9 3 *